"Every now and then... a book takes on a life of its own, a book that is passed down through the generations, one that becomes more valuable as the years pass by until one day you find the book in a museum or historical archives and it opens up the past like a magical portal. Do you Know your Mom's Story? by Glenna Mageau is that book. It contains 365 questions to ask your mother and in the process of gaining her answers, the book comes alive with her personality, her aspirations from her youth to her elder years, her plans, hopes, fears and experiences. And as her life unfolds, so does a snapshot in time of a place and an era that formed her world... it reaches far beyond dates of birth, marriage and death and into the heart and soul of a woman and her family..." Multi-Award-Winning Author P.M. Terrell

"A wonderful new self help book that masterfully inspires conversations between an adult child and his or her mother with genealogy. It's an important tool for adult children everywhere to have those conversations, to ask those questions of their mothers while they still can. The author provides insightful questions with thought provoking examples and explanations. It's a book about exploring one's heritage, strengthening or healing relationships and most importantly; honouring the wonderful person who brought you into this world. I love it!" Christine Jackson

"It reminded me of how much I don't know about my mom and it's giving me a glimpse into understanding why she made some choices she did in her life. This will be an interesting journey to do with Mom. What a great way to connect with her and get her story. Thank you." Sha B.

Do You Know Your Mom's Story?

365 Questions You Need to Ask Her

By

Glenna Mageau

First Edition: Published 2018

©Copyright Glenna Mageau 2018
All Rights Reserved.
Published by: Quadessence Press
Formatting: Patricia Terrell (P.I.S.C.E.S. Books)
Cover: Druscilla Morgan

ISBN: 9781775269816

Acknowledgements

To all Moms, you are inspiring women. Thank you for the beautiful role you chose to take on, it is not always easy, but it is full of gifts for you to reach out and embrace. Now it's time for you to share your story.

To my mom who was an inspiring woman who lost her way to her dreams but who has so inspired me to live mine. Thank you, Mom.

To all women, you truly are more powerful and more beautiful than you know.

To my family, Gerry, Jaz and Zack, you are my wings. Thank you. I love you.

To my Beta Team – Brenda, Christine, Sharon, Alisa, Helen, Jazmine, Patricia, Sylvia – your input is so incredibly appreciated and helpful. You are beautiful souls and I am grateful you are in my life.

To my siblings, I am forever grateful for you. You are the best gift.

To you my readers, you make my journey so worth it. Thank you, I couldn't do this without you. To all of you, may you grow, mend or heal your relationship with your mom and may you have an amazing journey through learning about her life.

Table of Contents

Your Mom's Information

My Mom (poem)

YOUR MOM's Information

Name at birth:

Name (if changed i.e. married):

Date of Birth:

Place of Birth:

Her eye color:

Her Parents:

Her Siblings:

Where does she fit in the lineup of siblings (1st, middle, last...):

My Mom

By Glenna Mageau

she held my hand when I couldn't walk

she gave me a push when I couldn't step forward

she was my safety net when I took a leap

she lifted me up when I lost my footing

she helped me to see beyond here and now

she opened the door for me to step through

she gave me the gift of me...

Chapter 1

Introduction

*Y*our mom has lived a full life and it's now time to discover her journey. I've suggested there are 365 questions you need to ask her but really you could probably ask a question a day for the rest of your life and still not learn all there is to know about this beautiful woman.

The purpose of this book is a way for you to grow, mend or heal your relationship with your mom along with learning her story. She may have seemed perfect to you or maybe she had a few flaws or maybe she was far from perfect but getting to know her can help you see her in a whole new light.

This book is so anyone can have the conversation with their mom about her life—learn who she was, who she is, what she has seen along the way, her hopes and dreams, her frustrations, her struggles, what had real meaning for her, what did she want most for you... It really is an in depth set of questions that will help you to document her story. To be honest though, I have geared this book towards getting that information from those Moms who are in their 70's, 80's, 90's, 100's... but it will work for capturing your mom's journey, no matter her age.

When I first started my career, I worked with seniors. I absolutely loved my job and I learned a lot. The biggest thing I discovered? We all want to know we matter—that we're seen, heard, understood and feel loved. Unfortunately, I discovered not too many seniors felt this way. I found that very sad. My goal is to change that, we should all feel that we are connected and be happy with our lives. My hope is you will really get to know your mom and to help her to have some connected, fulfilled days, weeks, months, years, before she leaves this world. But more than that, so you both can grow old and be at peace.

When we reach old age, we should be happy, healthy, loving life, know we made a positive difference, know we matter and to feel connected. If possible let's do that for our moms. I know not all relationships can be healed so if you can't heal your relationship with your mother, for whatever reason, then heal it from your perspective. Our relationships with our moms affect our lives in ways we can't often measure, so the more we are at peace with that connection, the healthier and happier we all will be.

Being a Mom is the most incredible gift and best role in the world, but it isn't the easiest. It's like being thrown into the CEO (Chief Executive Officer) of a new business without knowing a thing about it. So what do we do? We learn as we go. Unfortunately, there is a lot of work, pressure and expectation to get it right... the first time. In many cases it's like going into a dark tunnel and fumbling around 'til you find your way and pray you're headed in the right direction. Every Mom wants the best for their child. She wants for her child to do well but in the process of ensuring that happens, life gets busy and demanding and that want, can get grey and murky in all the chaos and all that is happening.

Our Moms are no different than we are—they had (and may still have) hopes, dreams, aspirations, good days, bad days, feeling they aren't worthy... — and if they grew up before the 60's they grew up in a time when women had certain expectations and roles they had to fulfill.

This book was inspired by two things. One, I got an opportunity to learn a lot about my own mom's journey, her dreams, her struggles and her regrets, before she left this world. I've documented some of it but it is scattered in different notebooks and on pieces of paper. I felt it was important to put all of her information together and the idea for this book came about. It was also inspired by some work I had been doing. I have been interviewing older women about their lives. They were women over the age of seventy, who stepped outside the norm for their day — they worked or got educated. They are some incredible women who have been very inspiring but who see their lives as just ordinary, not all that special. And sadly in some cases, they hadn't even shared a lot of what they had done in their lives with their own families. I found it so disheartening that this information would be lost. The family did not know and would not know this journey, this connection and have that understanding of who their mom was.

All moms need to have the opportunity to share their story, their journey. Being a Mom is the most amazing role in life, but it can be difficult and is often a thankless role. It truly has its own rewards but as a Mom if you aren't taught to look for those positives and are only taught to measure your worth by how your children show up in the world, then it is difficult to make that shift.

I truly hope you can ask your mom these questions while she is alive but if she has left this world, so you can't ask her directly, talk to other family members, friends, and some of the older people in your community who might know her. And read about the time and place she grew up in. See what you can learn.

Go into this quest with the understanding this isn't about you. Some of what you hear and some of the stories shared with you may surprise you, may make you laugh but some might hurt and make you feel unloved, unwelcome. Remember this is her journey and she is sharing what she knows and how she knows to share it. Do not take any of it personally. All she tells you and shares with you or decides not to share with you is from a woman who did what she knew, with what she had, in a time when she often had or got very little. Let her have her moment, see it with love and understanding and humor. Discover the journey she has been on and all she has learned. It truly is worth it.

If having this conversation with your mom just isn't possible for whatever reason, still try to get to know and understand her. It will help you to heal and to learn to forgive, even if you can't mend the relationship. At least you will know that you can approach old age differently than your mom did. You can know that you mattered, you can be happy, you can know you've made a positive difference and you can feel loved and connected.

I've included a lot of questions, but it is by no means a comprehensive list. Choose the ones that you feel are applicable and see what you can learn. They are in no particular order, so start where you feel works for you. This is a beginning to help you get the conversation started. There are so many things you will discover you can ask your mom and when she gets talking, keep asking and keep taking notes. Another option is to record your conversations. Just make sure that your mom is okay with that. You could have the recordings typed up for you. Also, if you have a number of siblings you might want to talk to each other. Try to coordinate getting this information so that you get it documented and so your mom doesn't feel overwhelmed with repeating the same stories. However, the truth is that each of you may also get different information from your mom, from the same questions. Talk to each other and share what you've learned so that you all can get a complete understanding of this beautiful woman, your mom.

After each conversation with your mom, be sure to reflect on all that she has shared with you. And before you start the next conversation with her, reflect on what you've learned, what you remember and what you'd like to learn. Make this a positive experience for both of you.

Chapter 2

Moms are Beautiful

$\mathcal{M}$oms are beautiful... this woman jumps into a role with no playbook, no rules and tries to wade through all the expectations that are out there. She's trying to figure out who she is, how to raise her kids to be healthy, whole and make a positive difference in the world, while juggling everything life throws at her. It is not easy. And as her kids we often just see her as Mom, the woman in our life who has guided us, who has pushed us, who has scolded us, who has tried to teach us, who's hope was to raise responsible, respectable children. Not really an easy task. She did what she knew with what she had.

Moms come in all shapes and sizes, beliefs, abilities, skills, knowledge... some became Moms because they wanted to, some reluctantly, while others didn't have a choice. Regardless of how or why she became a Mother, she really did want things to be better for you.

As children we often forgot she was human and had dreams and desires of her own. And may still have. We also didn't understand she grew up in a different time than us and how that has impacted her life. Just imagine all that you question, all that you feel is confusing and has put you in that place of not feeling you were good enough (cause we all do it) and go back in time to when your mom was growing up. Things were different. If she grew up before the 60's or 70's, there was little information out there about raising kids — except maybe, make sure they keep quiet and mind their manners. There was also a very different mindset about women — how they should be showing up and what they should and shouldn't be doing. It was also a time when you really didn't share your personal thoughts or ideas and you definitely didn't have access to all that is available now. So think about your life and all you learned from your mom and go back to when she was a child, guess who she learned from? Her mom, who grew up in a time of even more rules and oppression for women. Imagine being a woman who is taught the measure of who she is, depends on how her children show up in the world.

Understand that her childhood was a big part of developing her beliefs, habits and actions... a time that was very different to now. It's why it is so important to get to know her and understand her from the time when she grew up. What was she taught? What were the expectations? What did she really want? Time to step away from the role of Child and Mom and get to know this stranger who has been a part of your life... for a very long time.

Truthfully, there are about a million questions we need to ask our mom. She tells us a lot in our lifetime but how much do we really hear? Do we really remember? Do we really understand from her perspective or take the time to really get to know what she meant?

Did you ever find every now and then she'd do something that would surprise you? It seemed so out of character for her?

Well she just might have been exploring who she really is. Ask her about it.

Chapter 3

What do you really know about Your Mom?

We think we know our moms. We think we're pretty clear on who they are and what they want in life. But do we really? Do we really ask the questions of their life and how they lived, the ones that matter? And the biggest thing is do we listen? I know we hear them, even though Mom would say we probably didn't. Too often maybe we brush off what they say as repetitive or really not interesting or we see it as a put down. Or we listen but soon forget a lot of it. It truly all depends at what age we ask all of those questions, as well.

As a child we see our moms in certain ways—the caregiver, the discipliner, the one to run to when we have owies, the one who is always nagging us to do our chores... As a teenager we see our mom as our guide, the buffer from life, the one we blame for not being perfect, the one we ask everything, the one we ignore, the one we don't treat very well... We don't always respect her, but we do expect her to be there. We roll our eyes when she gives us unsolicited advice and promptly ignore it. As a young adult, we are often out to prove we know what we're doing and that we don't need help. At least not her help. We only ask questions when we really don't understand something. As we get older we start to see her differently, sometimes we want her advice and sometimes we want to show her we're now all grown up and we've figured things out on our own—when really, we haven't. The more we age, we start to understand her a whole lot more when we start having the same responsibilities she had. No matter our age we are always looking to see if she's the role model we want to follow or not. Or one that we've got something to prove to. Whichever it is, we are always looking for her approval. There is a part of us that needs to know we have her nod that we're doing okay. And of course, we are always looking for her love.

However you see your mom, my guess is you may not have really had a heart to heart with her about her... her life... her dreams... her aspirations... the things that went well... the things that didn't... how she handled the good and the bad... her proudest moment... her saddest moment... her beliefs about herself... her beliefs about life... what made her happy... what made her sad... does she have regrets... is there anything she'd do differently if she had the chance... her biggest life lesson... what she really wanted for you... where she feels she might have gotten lost...

Sometimes we've had parts of these conversations and other times we've gleaned information when she's shared because a situation has triggered a memory but too often we assume too much. We don't really probe or really take it all in. And sometimes she just won't share. Sometimes it is just too painful for her, possibly because she doesn't see it as important... because she feels as though she has failed... or maybe because she doesn't feel she has done enough... mattered enough...

Having a conversation with your mom can be difficult, especially if there is frustration, anger and past hurts underlying your relationship. Or if your mom sees her life as not important or something that needs to be left in the past and therefore she won't share.

It can be difficult to have this talk with her, but it is important to start. Going through this book and getting the answers to her life will be a gift to you and to her but know it is not meant to be done all at once. It would be too overwhelming for her and for you. This is your opportunity to connect with her on a different level. When you get into this, she may say some stuff you've heard before but hopefully she'll tell you some new information. You may also hear things you want to hear and some things you don't. The best advice I can give you is don't take it personally. Just listen, ask questions, probe when she answers but stay out of your own stuff and do not judge her. She made decisions based on what she knew with what was available to her.

Finding out about her journey is about discovering who she really is and how she saw the world as a young child to that of where she's at now. She is going back in time so the way she is telling the story, what she recalls or what she thinks she might have wanted at a certain age, may have changed. She may also not share everything with you. Some things might be too hard for her to talk about and she may have suppressed some things long enough she won't remember.

The key to this is to start the conversation and open up the doors to discovering this woman who is your mother.

Chapter 4

Being a Mom

Your mom, she is the woman you love but sometimes push away. Sometimes you seek her help, but sometimes you don't want any advice from her. In fact, often you'll do the opposite of what she says. And as a mom you are expected to know what to do, when to do it and how to do it... no matter what. But let's be honest we are all doing what we can with what we know. Our moms were the same but most of them did it in a time when things were very different.

Love her. She may not have done everything perfect or even well, but she did what she knew. I'm pretty sure every mother's goal is for her children to have a better life than she did. Just about everything your mom has been done has been aimed at achieving that goal. Sometimes it might have been clear to you and other times you may feel it is not the truth at all. I do know we hold our moms to a higher standard, we expect a lot. I just want you to understand the person she is— understand who she is, what she has done, what she wanted to do and why she made the decisions she did. Remember things were very different when she grew up. It's a time that may have passed but it influenced her life on a very deep level.

Our moms lived in kind of an awkward period. If your mom raised you in the 50's, 60's or 70's, it had to be somewhat difficult. It was a time of change. Everyone seemed tired of the shut down way of being, especially for women. There were a lot of people trying to make positive changes. Even with all the strides to break free of the old — the old rules, the old manners, the old thoughts about men and women and their roles, the old ways of being — it still carried forward into a lot of what we were taught as children.

Today we are in a time of rapid change, more so than at any other time in history. We are also in a time where pretty much everything is shared and is out there to be discussed. Well when your mom was growing up that wasn't the case. Things were often kept hushed, you didn't share them in public, in fact you did what you could to hide them. Many things weren't talked about openly and there is no denying history has not treated women all that well or respected them very much. Your mom has overcome a lot of adversity — some of it she is aware of and some was just built into the societal norms. She has gone through a lot in her lifetime, learn what it is.

This woman who raised you is amazing... but not perfect. Change the conversations you have with her. Let her know she is important to you on a different level, that you want to know who she is. By helping her to look at her life and the positives of all she has done and been through, you just might help her to realize the gift she is.

Women are beautiful, smart, funny and amazing caregivers but often forget to honor themselves. Help your mother realize her life mattered... that she matters... give her the gift of understanding.

Ask these questions over time. And ask them again and again but in a different way and in different situations. Each time you might learn something new, a new memory may come to mind for your mom. Some of these questions will apply and some won't, and some your mom just might not want to answer or maybe can't remember.

Have fun with this and use it not only to gather information but to understand how this woman was raised and how she views the world and why she views it that way. With this you'll always have a guide, the material that one day you just won't be able to ask her any more. Believe me it is the toughest day when you realize you can no longer ask your mom how to do things... who is so and so... how did she make... what does she think of... just to talk to her... to ask her...

Honor your mom, she took the most rewarding and toughest role in the world and did what she knew with what she had.

Chapter 5

The Time Your Mom Grew Up In

*L*et me take you back in time. Your mom grew up in a very discrete generation, especially if she grew up before the 60's. The mentality, the lifestyle, the beliefs, and the knowledge were very different than it is now. For instance, the aspirations for women were pretty much second, third or nonexistent. Women were really taught to do as told, look after others and when they grew up, to get married and have kids. Even if your mom was one of the women who stepped outside the norm, and worked or got educated, society still had that mentality. It was there around every corner reminding women it was going to be that much harder, there were going to be that many more rules for them to follow. There were so many standards for women to uphold. Did you know in some professions if a woman got married, she had to quit her job? In other professions if she wasn't married she couldn't work? If she was pregnant, she couldn't work?

It was also in a time when things were becoming automated but lots still had to be done by hand—from doing dishes (and in big families that was a big deal), to doing laundry, ironing (because your clothes had to look just so), to having a huge garden, to putting food on the table, to heating the house… —it was a lot of work. Your mom worked hard, tried to keep everything up to the standards, raise kids in the best way she knew how, and she was expected to do it without complaining. Emotions were something that weren't expressed a lot, at least not sadness and tears. Even laughter seemed to be limited.

The truth is no matter what kind of life women lived back when your mom was raised, there was a real subservient expectation for women and it would have been very hard not to adopt it. So what did that mean for your mom? It meant she learned she had to shut down her emotions and if she really wanted to do well, she had good manners and was sure others' needs were met first. It meant she had to close off part of who she was, who she is, and she had to distance herself from her feelings. Why? Because they made her look weak and really served no purpose... at least that's how emotions seemed to have been perceived. There was a lot of work to be done and feeling sad or lonely just got in the way.

You have this woman, who is no different than you —she wants to know that she has done her best and is appreciated. To be strong she had to take whatever came at her and keep going. She had to show she could take it all on. When she got married and had kids, she had to make sure her kids understood the importance of manners and how to show up in public—image was very important. It measured how good you were. She was never hard on you because she didn't like you, but she had to make sure you learned the 'rules' because that also meant she was doing the right thing and doing what was expected and raising you properly. Unfortunately for the kids, it often translated into not being enough, not being good enough, not being worthy… Hence the yearning for Mom's love, Mom's acceptance and Mom's respect.

Don't get me wrong there were several moms who got this right, who knew how to say I love you, how to give a hug, how to be gentle and caring but there were those who did not. They tried to play by the rules, they tried to find themselves and maybe they tried to change the rules but got lost in what all that meant. And many of these women got lost in their fears and their beliefs that they weren't enough. And they had no one to talk to about it. You did not share you were feeling lost or not enough. No one wanted to hear it. It was considered self-pity and there was no time for that stuff.

What does it mean for you in trying to build a relationship with this woman who raised you? It means you need to understand where she was coming from when you were little and where she's at now. Imagine living the perfect life as it has been laid out for you, trying to follow the guidelines, trying to make some positive changes but always feeling judged and not worthy. You did all you thought you were supposed to and still felt empty and disconnected with who you are. Having shut down your emotions for most of your life, you are now reaching an elderly age, would you even want to go near those feelings? Especially if all you learned is they were pointless, would hurt and keep you lost? What would you do with them at this point in your life?

Chapter 6

What is Your Relationship?

Connecting with your mom is one of the most rewarding gifts but can also be the most difficult thing to do. It all depends on your relationship with her. If you were/are fortunate to have a loving, giving, open and receiving relationship with your mom be sure to treasure it because it is a type of relationship a lot of people did not and do not have.

Many adult children just accept the relationship with Mom as is without realizing it can be changed. Too often as adult children we believe we have tried to connect, to get her love, to get her approval but she stays the same. And she very likely will but... you can change. Before you get mad and think, I'm always the one trying to do things to make it work, there are a few tips that might help with altering your relationship. How you approach your mom can make all the difference. Too often we come from where we are at, from what we know and believe today, and can't figure out how come she can't show her emotions more or why she can't change her attitude. The truth is that in many cases if she had, she wouldn't have made it to the age she is and she might not have survived all she went through.

Your relationship with your Mom falls into at least one of these categories, depending on the situation and sometimes the day:

1. A loving, giving, mutually respectful relationship

2. A friend-type relationship

3. An intellectual relationship - you have good conversations but not personal ones

4. An emotional relationship - more of a push and pull

5. A superficial relationship - you talk about the weather, the neighbors...

6. Barely speaking - more of an avoidance relationship, you don't share personal information, if at all possible

7. Not speaking

It doesn't matter how old you are—6 or 65—there is this need to feel loved, accepted, respected and have your mom's approval. It is something all children strive for. It's kind of an odd feeling when you are a mature, independent adult and you realize you still have that yearning, that need. It is normal though and really shows how important it is to a child, no matter their age. Sometimes you know you have love and acceptance from your mom. Or you feel you may be able to work towards getting it and having her show it to you. Or you may realize it just isn't going to happen because she can't. Which probably means she never got it. Whatever happens with your relationship, you need to come to peace with it... for your sake. Do what you can to heal it but also know, you are enough. You are a beautiful, smart, loved child. Your mom just might not have been or be able to show you... at least not in the way you need.

Remember she grew up in a very different time with different expectations, understandings and ways of expressing love or caring.

Chapter 7

Your Mom's Love Language

How do you know if your mom loves you?

It seems like an easy enough question and the simple answer would be she tells you, 'I love you', right? Unfortunately, it isn't or maybe wasn't something she said or showed too much.

I've talked about the fact your mom grew up in a different time. She grew up in a time when emotions weren't really encouraged, and neither was physical touching. She might not have learned how to say, 'I love you'. She also may not have been one to touch you much, other than to put a band-aid on your cut or to put her hand to your forehead when you were sick, to see if you were hot or not. On occasion when you were little, she might have taken your hand when you were walking. I'm not going to get into all the reasons why you didn't hear it or feel that love the way you needed to, but it was the norm in many homes and cultures. And still is in some.

The truth is your mom probably never heard 'I love you' from her parents... or anyone. Today, it is quite normal and natural to say, 'I love you' and to give a hug. Your mom might have even learned how to do that, which is awesome but if not and she didn't do these things when you were a kid, does it mean she didn't love you? Unfortunately, I think too often that's how we, the kids saw it. We often wondered and would look for those moments of a soft touch or praise, which could also be few and far between. It was more often than not the lack of getting in trouble that was the key we were on Mom's good side.

So how did Mom express her love? Her caring? And believe me she did. Some moms showed loved by giving you a hug, kissing you, saying I love you but for many moms, doing the manual things around the house for the family—cooking; cleaning (which could take a long time); doing laundry; ironing; gardening; maybe going to work to make money; guiding you to do more or be more; making you things to use or to play with; ensuring you had clothes, food...; teaching you skills—were just some of the things she did that were her way of expressing her love.

Think back to your childhood. What were some of the things that your mom did for you?

> Did your mom make you a special meal? Some special cookies? Or a cake?
> Did your mom make sure your clothes looked good, clean, mended?
> Did your mom make your clothes?
> Did your mom clean your room? Make your bed?
> Did your mom do your laundry?
> Did your mom keep a garden?
> Did your mom show up at all of your events?
> Did your mom push you to get involved in different activities?

I know it may not feel like that was love but it was. It was her way of showing she cared and it was what was an accepted way of expressing emotion. For some reason it seemed that stating your feelings was seen as wrong or as a weakness. You just didn't share your emotions.

Think back to the little things she used to do with you and for you.

> Did she read to you?
> Did she do crafts with you?
> Did she take you on hikes? Out in nature?
> Did she take you to special places?
> What were the little things she used to do either with you or for you?
> Did she encourage you to try new things?
> Did she get on your case to practice? Do your homework?
> Did she teach you new skills?
> Did she shoo you outside to spend time in nature? To go do something?
> What were some of the things she did with you?
> Did she enrol you in some lessons?
> Sometimes she let you know she cared by the questions she asked... over... and over...

We don't tend to see those things as anything but what a Mom is supposed to do. That's her job. True to some degree but she also had a lot going on, had to work very hard and had to make sure everything was taken care of but most importantly she had you. And she did it all without many of the modern conveniences we have today. She was showing she cared for you in the best way she knew how and still be able to keep on top of everything.

Sometimes she might have been trying to discover if she was loved. She may not have heard it in her lifetime from an adult, never mind her children. Moving forward, let her know you do love her. Tell her often 'I love you' but also tell her 'I love you' and give it a moment of silence and if possible with a hug or a held hand so she can really feel it and so can you. You might just be amazed at how much it truly means to her and to you. If you truly can't do that because you just don't have that kind of relationship or the possibility of it, then imagine it happening. Imagine having that loving, giving moment and make it your truth about your relationship. Why? Because it will help to heal you and those old wounds you might be carrying around.

If you are trying to connect with your mom today, try to approach her through the things she likes to do, to watch... But also try to show her the things that have meaning for you, just don't expect her to love what you are telling her or what you like. She has gotten to a stage in life where she is getting comfortable with her life and doesn't want a whole lot of change. Honor that, it doesn't mean you can't show her new stuff or give her new experiences just know she may not be interested in doing it again. It has nothing to do with you but with the fact she likes the calm, controlled world she's created and doesn't want to change it. She's finally got some peace in her life and doesn't feel like she's being told which direction to go and how to do it.

Remember, going into old age is about being happy, healthy, loved and connected, and to do that you need to heal. Her story is as much about you as it is your mom.

Chapter 8

How and When to Talk to Your Mom

How and when you talk to your mom can make all the difference in what you learn and experience.

Deciding to talk to your mom is a big step, especially about her journey—where she was and where she is at now. It is important to remember this might be an emotional roller coaster for her and for you.

When you decide to sit down and ask your mom about her life, make sure you are gentle with her. Start with those things that will get her talking but aren't all that personal. If you know of there are some topics she doesn't like sharing, or you've seen her get mad when someone has mentioned a certain time in her life, do not start there. Often asking where and when she was born is a good place to open the conversation but it all depends on whether it was a traumatizing time or not.

Sometimes it is good to be direct and just tell her you'd like to learn about her journey, about who she is. However, for some women this is really tough for them to talk about themselves or to share their life. If this is the case, you'd be better to ask her questions in an indirect way. Wait until you are doing an activity or you're talking about something you know might relate to her past or that you can relate to her past in some way. Compare and contrast today to her youth — what are the differences and the similarities. Which does she prefer?

For example, if you know she loves watching skating, ask her questions.

> Did you ever skate? Where did you skate? What got you started? How good were you? When was the last time you went? Who did you like to skate with? What is your fondest memory of skating? Where did you like to go skating? What was it like? What were your skates like? What do you think of the skates nowadays compared to what you used? It's pretty amazing what they can do on skates now, did you ever try spins or jumps?

Do not ask all these questions at one time. Ask one, let her answer and then keep probing with another question.

If you're struggling to get her to talk about herself or her life, take her to some events she'd enjoy or to some place you know she likes or out for lunch and just ask casual questions. 'Did she have anything like this when she was a child?' or 'How did they do that when she was young?' Fit the conversation into the situation you are in. Really, she wants to share but she may not know how so create opportunities for her that take the direct focus off of her.

The other thing you can do is to give her this book and ask her to go through the questions and to write out what she remembers about her life. She might find that easier to do. Be sure to ask her every now and then though, about some of the memories she has written. Try to get her to talk to you about it. Ask if you can read what she has written. She may let you, but she may not, so don't make a big deal out of it. Encourage her to keep writing, just understand it might be a cathartic journey or it could be a difficult one for her.

Your mother is an amazing woman, but she may not know it. All women are amazing, but Moms really do hold a special place. The truth is being a Mom is a journey and not always an easy one. There is so much to do and really there is no 'rule book' on how you are to raise this little one that is now so dependent on you.

Today there is so much information for new moms and support but think back to before the '70's, there was not a lot of information. Women were expected to have children and raise them and know what they were doing. And although the ladies would talk about raising kids and some of the things that happened, they really didn't seek advice from each other. At least not too often. It doesn't mean advice wasn't given, it just may not have been wanted. Often your mom only had herself to rely on with raising you and however many other children she had. She may have had some support and been able to talk to your father and have him help but more often than not, a lot fell on her shoulders. Often, she had to wade through it on her own.

Prior to having kids though, this woman had dreams and aspirations and ideas about where her life was going. Do you know what those were? Do you know how your mom felt about being a mother? This isn't about digging up dirt or finding a reason to get mad at your mom, but it is a way to get to know her and understand her a bit better.

This could be an sensitive journey for your mom which might be why she's reluctant to share it. It may open old hurt that she hasn't healed. Be there for her, understand her, give her the love and support she needs and let her know you understand. Take your time but find a way to talk to her, it will be worth it.

Chapter 9

To Really Connect, Go Back in Time

To connect to your mom, you need to go back in time, to her time, to when she grew up. It is when she is most connected to. Find those things that have meaning for her, those things she knows from when she was young and growing up. Start with generic things she can relate to—the telephone, doing laundry, transportation, community events... It might mean you need to learn some history—what was going on when she was a child, what were the conditions like, how did they heat their homes, how did they cook, where did they get their food, what did they get paid, how did they get around, what did they use for transportation, how did they do laundry, how did they communicate long distance, what was the community like, what was the weather like, what was school like, where did they get their clothes, what were the expectations of women (in her words), what was the political world like... No matter what generation she grew up in things have and do change very fast. Technology and all we do, how we do it and all we use, has changed a lot over the years.

Talk about the similarities and the differences in the times. What does she think about the progress? What does she miss from her old days?

Once you've got the conversations started, then get into more personal ones. What did she love to do as a child? What was it like growing up? There are many questions in this book you can start asking her but know it's not just about getting her information down on paper, it is about understanding her and who she is and who she was. Some things have changed a lot for her and some not as much. What tends to be a bit slower in changing, is the attitude, beliefs and habits that we all carry forward. They get passed on from generation to generation. Each time we strive to do better and be better but although there are a lot of changes in our physical world, it takes longer for us to shift how we see, act and react to each other. So it might take her a while to understand that sharing her journey is a good thing.

Something you can do to start or to expand the conversation with your mom is to not only listen to her journey but to share some of your experiences and your story—your doubts, your worries, your issues… Share about yourself. Let her see some of your vulnerabilities, some of your struggles, some of your understandings about life. You might be reluctant as you might think she'll judge you and might say something that hurts you. If that is a concern, start the conversation with telling her you want to share with her, but you don't want a negative response from her. See how she reacts. And ask her, 'Did she want to connect to her mom but didn't know how?' If you get a positive reaction, try it. Start with the telling her the easy stuff, the stuff that won't hurt if she knows it. If she does say something hurtful, you will know you can't go this route, at least not fully. Hopefully you will be able to get some discussion happening to where you can connect on a deeper, more personal level.

When you talk to her, go in with no expectations and an open mind. Talk to her like you would a stranger and use all those manners she taught you. It truly can be really eye-opening and a lot of fun. But if you are feeling some anxiety or worrying about old patterns, take a deep breath, and step out of your hurt, pain and frustration with her. If you hold onto all she didn't give you as a child, as a young adult, as an adult, you may not understand who she is and you may not mend this relationship. When I say mend, I mean from your perspective.

These questions are but a tool to help you to get to know this woman. Hopefully it will help you to come to some sort of peace with who she is and how she raised you and the relationship you have or don't have.

There are many ways to approach talking with your mom and with getting her history, but you may have to be patient and nurturing. She may need to know you aren't going to take her information and judge her. Unfortunately, she may feel that way. It might be like your reluctance to share with her. She might be where you learned it from.

Think back to when you were young and how much things have changed from then to now. Add another 20 years or so to that and imagine all the changes your mom has seen in her lifetime. Change isn't something many of us tolerate well, so just think of the huge shift in everything you know from the growth in the size of the communities; to drastic changes in transportation; to the different styles of clothes; to the ways and opportunities to travel; technology; the cost of everything; to contacting and connecting with someone— cell phones, text messages, email; to social media—sharing everything that was kept private...

Things are miles apart from when she was a child.

Chapter 10

Asking the Questions

Asking the questions on the following pages will help you to get to know your mom and have a whole new understanding and appreciation for her and her life.

There are so many ways to approach talking with your mother, from outright asking questions to doing it subtly as situations arise. When you have a conversation with her to start learning about her journey, where you start will depend on three things: the relationship you have with your mom; how ready you are to hear some of it; and how ready your mom is to talk about it.

It is important to know there is information she may not want to share with you. Be okay with it. Some things might be too difficult for her to discuss with you—privacy, guilt, shame, not feeling good enough, not wanting to hurt you or others, doesn't feel it would help anything, she doesn't see it as important... If she doesn't want to talk about a subject you can ask her why and she might tell you—she feels guilt... shame... it would hurt you...—but she may not. The purpose of this is not to offend her or to make her mad or to have her withdraw from you, so if she refuses to tell you anything, let it go. Just let her know that you don't judge her and only want to get to know her and her journey. Let her know that you understand and respect her decision but if she ever changes her mind, you'd love to hear about her life.

If she won't answer direct questions about her life or says, 'I don't want to talk about me', then wait until you're in a situation to bring it up in conversation and switch to asking general questions. If you can prepare for your time with her—and do some homework so you know some of the history of the time when she grew up, the more you will be able to draw out of her.

> "Mom did you ever eat pizza as a kid? Did they have pizza places?"

> "Mom, what was the first phone like that your family had? Was it a party line?"

> "When did you learn to drive? Who taught you? What type of vehicle was it?"

As I mentioned we all want to know we matter, if your mom is reluctant to talk about herself or her life, recognize it is a lifetime of learning that has shut her down. The truth is you may have a difficult time getting her to talk but even if you only have superficial conversations about the weather always try to take it back to when she was young. You can ask things like, what was the worst storm she ever saw? What were they doing when it hit and how did they manage to get through it? You can learn a lot about her life through this.

The one big thing you can do for this beautiful woman, whether you heal the relationship with her or not, or feel you aren't getting much from her, is to tell her you are grateful for her. Let her know you understand she had a lot to deal with and that it couldn't have been easy. To help her to see the positive, give some examples of some of the good things she did for you from when you were kids… teens… adult… Again, be prepared for any response from her because it might be a good one but it might not be. She may accept what you say and show she is touched by it, or she might acknowledge you've told her but not really express much or she may push it away and ignore it. Even though what you say is positive, she might not be able to accept that admiration. But know that she heard you, she just can't go there. Taking praise or being recognized for who she was and what she did are probably not something she has heard much, if at all. She really may not know how to respond. Emotions were something that probably didn't serve her well in her lifetime, so for her to start expressing them or to step back into sentiment or gratitude, might just not be possible. The truth is she probably hasn't learned how to say something positive when she gets praise, so you can take this time to teach her. Simply tell her what you need from her, 'Mom, I need you to say thank you when I do this…', 'Mom, I'd really like if you'd stop saying…'. This is what I'd like to hear you say…'

Be gentle, be kind and do not take it personally if she is gruff or can't express what you ask. Just keep reminding her, gently. She is doing what she knows and just like the rest of us, she doesn't like change. She wants a life of peace and one where she is in her comfort zone. It might not be one that you like but it is where she feels safe and is in the most in control. Recognize that as it might help you to shift from seeing it as a slight against you.

I've laid out the questions so they are by topic but they are really in no particular order. Start where you feel you need to and with the questions that are relevant to your Mom's life. I've also provided some blank pages after each section for you to write down the stories she shares. There are more blank pages at the end of the book so that you can capture more of her information and memories.

This is your journal of your mom's life, enjoy the journey.

Chapter 11

The Fun and Interesting Stuff

Too often, we forget our moms had a life before us, she had hopes and dreams and did things. It's time to find out a bit more about her. Get to know what she enjoyed doing and what were some of the interesting things that happened in her life. This is just a fun snapshot of a few highlights of her life.

What are some of the fun/interesting events in her life? In her childhood? Tweens? Teens? In her 20's? 30's? 40's? 50's? 60's? 70's? 80'? 90's? 100's?

Did she seek out fun/interesting things to do? or if they happened they happened?

Who did she have the most fun with?

What were things she saw as fun?

What made her laugh?

Did she laugh much?

Did her family like to laugh?

Did she ever do something daring? Or want to? Did she ever climb a tree?

What's the funnest thing she ever did? What was the most interesting thing she ever did?

Who was her first kiss? Her first love?

What did she get in trouble for? How did it come about?

What was the best part of her childhood?

Who did she want to be when she was young?

What was her favorite song when younger? What is her favorite song now?

What was her favorite book/story as a child? As an adult? Now?

What activities/sports did she enjoy as a child? Tweens? Teen? 20's? 30's? 40's? 50's? 60's? 70's? 80's? 90's? 100's? Which were her favorite?

Did she have a favorite toy as child?

Did she wear makeup as a teenager? What did her parents think? Was it the norm? Or was she doing something most women didn't?

When did she learn to drive? Who taught her?

What would she change if she could go back in time?

What education did she get? Why did she take the level of education she did?

Did she ever work? How much did she get paid? What kind of work and what kind of hours did she have to work? What was her boss like?

What is she most proud of?

What is something she always wanted to do or to learn but didn't?

What's the most embarrassing moment in her life?

What was/is her favorite flower?

What was/is her favorite food?

What was/is her favorite smell?

What was/is her favorite color?

Did she have a pet as a child? Adult? What was it? What was its name?

Notes/Stories

Notes/Stories

Notes/Stories

Notes/Stories

Notes/Stories

Chapter 12

When Your Mom was Born

Her Birth

Birth is something that is magical, unexplainable and to be truthful it can be quite painful. It is not an easy process, for some it isn't too bad but for other women it is very difficult and lengthy. Even if that's true, it is something most women wouldn't change it and it is soon forgotten because the outcome is perfect... you, their new baby. So beautiful. Women have been having babies forever, it's not something modern. What is new is how we see and approach pregnancy and having babies and the access to medical or specialized care—something that was somewhat limited when your mom had you. Now go back to when her mom had her, to the day your mom was born. Wow, things were very different then. Look it up and see what was going on for women having children in those days and specifically where—the town, city, country— your mom was born and raised.

Before the 70's, being pregnant was something that was private and not really shared. To be pregnant was exciting but in many ways, it was also seen a woman's duty to have a baby. It was okay to be pregnant and have babies it just wasn't okay for others to see you when you started to grow and show. There was also a bit of shame in what having a growing baby inside of you, did to your body. So these women got pregnant but really had no one to talk to about it. Sometimes they had their moms and sometimes they had friends they could ask but it wasn't something that was often openly discussed. And women who were far along in their pregnancies, didn't go out in public very much. Just imagine all you are going through as this baby is growing inside of you and you have no one to talk to about it. The bigger you got, the more you had to hide it. You were not really able to share that joy and the fear of having a baby and what it all meant, with really anyone.

Really ask questions about her birth, what she knows about it and what was life like in those days. Also ask her about when she had you, what was it like and what were the times like. Compare that to the present day, it's truly quite different.

Now think about what her mom had to do for diapers, cleaning, food, clothing… There was no running to the store to get supplies like diapers or canned baby food… there wasn't often even a washing machine… running water… Can you imagine the work involved in having one baby, let alone several?

> What was your Mom's name at birth? How did she get her name?

> What is her current name (if changed i.e. due to marriage)?

> What is her date of birth?

> What time of the day was she born?

> What is her astrological sign?

Where was she born? What town/city, province/state, country?

Where exactly was she born—in hospital, at home, enroute, other?

Was there anything unique about her birth?

Were there any complications with her birth?

How was her mother's pregnancy? Were there any issues, anything unique that happened during the pregnancy?

If she had siblings, how did they feel about having a new baby sister?

What has she been told about how she was as a baby?

Did she have any birth marks?

Where did she sleep as a baby? (crib, dresser drawer, in bed with parents...)

Did her parents have a high chair for her? Or did they stack books for her to sit on?

Did her parents have a stroller or buggy that they used with her?

What was it like back in the times when her mom was pregnant with her? How was child-bearing viewed? Were women choosing not to have children? Not to have as many children? Not getting married? Were women starting to step outside the norm and work or get educated?

What kind of medical support was there? Did her mom ever need any?

Was her dad able to be present? Or anyone else?

Did they have a special ceremony? Or celebration?

How did her mom carry her around—in a sling? In her arms?...?

Did they have any pets? Did her mom ever worry about having animals around her?

What kind of food did her mom feed her as a baby? Toddler? Child?

What kind of clothes did she wear as a baby? Toddler? Child? Where did her mom get her clothes (i.e. buy them, borrow them, sew them, hand-me-downs…)?

What was something special her mom liked to do with her as a baby? Toddler? Child?

What was something special her dad liked to do with her as a baby? Toddler? Child?

Was there anyone else special to her when she was a child?

What was the funnest story about her childhood?

Did she have a favorite stuffed animal? Toy?

Was there a special story her mom or dad used to tell her? Or song they sang to her?

Notes/Stories

Notes/Stories

Notes/Stories

Notes/Stories

Notes/Stories

Notes/Stories

Chapter 13

Her Upbringing

What was her upbringing?

Understanding more about her background, where she was raised, how she was raised, the beliefs she was raised with, the rules, how her family interacted… all will help to give a better picture of her, her life and who she is.

Where did your mom grow up? In the country (rural)? In the city (urban)?

Did she have pets growing up? If yes, what? Their names? What was special about her pets?

What is her favorite memory of growing up?

Did she have a nickname? How did she get it? Did she like it? Is she still called that? By whom?

What kind of things did she do as a child? By herself? With her siblings? With her parents? With others?

How many siblings did she have? What were their names? Their age? Did they get along? What were some fun things they used to do?

What did they like to do as a family? Did they play games? Sports? Do other activities? What? How often?

Was she from an artistic family? What kind of things did they do—paint, draw, write, sculpt, hobbies, crafts, etc.?

Was she from an athletic family? What kind of sports/activities did she do? Did they do?

Did they ever attend a special event—a show, a musical event…?

What is her least favorite memory of growing up?

Did she have to do chores? What chores?

Was she close to her mom and dad? One more than the other?

Was she close to her siblings?

Where does your mom fit in the lineup of children—first, middle, last, fifth...?

What were her responsibilities regarding the family, the household and her siblings, growing up? (i.e. babysitter, clothes washer, cook, etc.)

Did she enjoy spending time with her parents? Siblings?

What were meals like? What did they usually eat? Who cooked? Who cleaned up? Where did they eat? Were there any rituals they did?

What is something that was in the house she grew up in that she has a distinct memory of? What meaning did it hold for her?

What was it like in the neighborhood she grew up in?

What were the expectations for your mom's life? From her parents? Her community?

What were some of their family traditions?

Did her parents play sports? If yes what?

Were her parents musically inclined?

Were her parents artistic?

Did her parents belong to any clubs or have memberships?

What did her parents like to do in their free time? Did they have any hobbies?

Did she ever get into trouble? What was she doing? What happened? Did she ever do it again?

What did she spend a lot of her time doing? As a child? Tween? Teen? Young Adult?

What were things she liked to do her parents disapproved of?

Did she ever hide things from her parents?

What does she think her parents wanted for her in life?

Today or maybe for a good part of her life, does she still do any of the activities she learned while growing up?

Who did she talk to about problems? As a child? Tween? Teen? Young adult?

Did her and her family do things in the community? What? Where? How frequently?

How did her family celebrate special occasions—Holidays/ Statutory Holidays, Birthdays, Anniversaries, Special Occasions...?

Did she feel she fit in with her family?

Did she feel her parents were there for her?

Did she feel her siblings were there for her?

Did she ever date? Was she allowed to date when living at home?

How did her parents feel about her dating? Her siblings dating?

Who was her first love?

What would she change about her childhood, if she could?

What did she fear as a child? Why?

What was the house like she grew up in? Did they ever move?

How far away was the nearest neighbor?

What was it like in the neighborhood she grew up in?
Were there a lot of community events? What were they? Did her family attend?

Did they ever go on a vacation as a family? If yes, to where? How did they travel?

Where does she believe she got her strength from, over the years, to deal with all that occurred in her life?

Was she closer to her mom or her dad? Why?

What were some of the rules she was raised with?

What was her favorite food?

Did she ever have candy when she was young? Did they make it or buy it?

Did she learn to ride a bike? Did she own one? Who taught her? Funniest moment when learning to ride?

Did she learn to ride a horse? Did she own one? Who taught her? Funniest moment when learning to ride?

Did she learn how to drive? Who taught her? Funniest moment when learning to drive?

Notes/Stories

Notes/Stories

Notes/Stories

Notes/Stories

Notes/Stories

Notes/Stories

Notes/Stories

Chapter 14

Her Family
Parents, Their Siblings, Grandparents

*P*art of understanding your mom and getting to know more about her, is to get to know more about her parents, her grandparents, her aunts and uncles…

Who are your mom's parents (your grandparents)? What were their names? Where did they live? What did they do? What can she tell you about them? Did she ever meet them?

Did her parents have siblings? If yes, who were they? Did your mom get along with the aunts and uncles? Who did she like? Not like? What about her cousins—who did she like? Not like? Did they do any fun things together?

What is her mom's story—when and where born, upbringing, education, work, life lived, type of person (happy, strict, giving, caring, community minded, religious...), parents, siblings?

What is her dad's story—when and where born, upbringing, education, work, life lived, type of person (happy, strict, giving, caring, community minded, religious...), parents, siblings?

Did your dad have siblings (your aunts and uncles)? How would your mom describe them—happy, strict, quiet, smart, practical, loving, giving, caring, community minded, reclusive, hard working...? Did she get along with the in-laws?

Did your mom have siblings (your aunts and uncles)? How would your mom describe her siblings—happy, strict, quiet, smart, practical, loving, giving, caring, community minded, reclusive, hard working...? Did she get along with them?

Did either her mother's or father's side have family reunions? If yes, what were they like? How many would attend? Where would they hold it? How often did they have them? If not, did they have regular family get togethers? How many would attend? Where would they hold it?

Did they visit the grandparents or aunts and uncles, cousins? How frequently?

Did she get along with her cousins? Doing anything special?

Was there anyone unique or different or someone who did something unique or different in her parents' family?

Notes/Stories

Notes/Stories

Chapter 15

Marriage/Relationships

How people meet and get married is often quite fascinating. Sometimes they've known each other since babies, sometimes it's by chance that they meet and sometimes there is quite a story as to how they met. Through the years the process of meeting and getting married has changed somewhat. In the past, some women and men fell in love and chose to get married, some were told to get married and some it was arranged for them. Do you know the story of how your parents met? How they fell in love… How the proposal came about… Where they got married… Did they stay married… You might find out some interesting information. You can also ask your mom about her parents and their relationship and how it came about.

Her Parents

How did her parents meet? How old were they?

What attracted her mom to her dad? Was it an arranged marriage? Or by choice?

How long did they date before getting married? What was their courtship like?

What kind of work did her father do when they met? Did his work/career change at all over the years?

How did the marriage proposal happen?

When did they get married? What date? What age were they when they got married?

Where did they get married?

What was her mom's wedding dress like? Did she keep it?

Did her mom get an engagement ring? A wedding ring? If yes, what did they look like? How did she feel about them? What happened to her wedding rings? If no, what did she get to signify she was married?

Did her mom give her dad a wedding ring? Why or why not?

Was her wedding what she always dreamed it would be? Did she keep any mementos?

When did they decide to have children?

How many children did they have (how many siblings do you have)?

What is a special memory of their relationship?

Did they stay married? Why? Or why not? How long were they married?

Your Parents

How did your parents meet? How old were they?

What attracted your mom to your dad? How long did they date before getting married? What was their courtship like? Was it an arranged marriage?

Was it love at first sight?

How did her parents feel about their relationship? How did his parents feel about their relationship?

What kind of work did your father do when they met? Did his work/career, change at all over the years?

How did the marriage proposal happen?

When did they get married? What date? How old were they when they got married?

Where did they get married?

What was her wedding dress like? Did she keep it?

Did she get an engagement ring? A wedding ring? If yes, what did they look like? How did she feel about them? If no, what did she get to signify she was married?

Did she give your dad a wedding ring? Why or why not?

Was her wedding what she always dreamed it would be? Did she keep any mementos?

When did they decide to have children?

How many children did they have (how many siblings do you have)?

What is a special memory of their relationship?

Did they stay married? Why? Or why not? How long were they or have they been married?

What were and are your mom's beliefs about marriage?

What does your mom think is key to a successful marriage?

Notes/Stories

Notes/Stories

Notes/Stories

Notes/Stories

Chapter 16

What was her Education?

Today we don't think much about getting an education, at least primary and secondary (elementary to high school) and even on to post secondary (university, college, trades) but in your mom's day it wasn't always the case. Sometimes the school was too far away, sometimes the kids had to be boarded with another family, sometimes correspondence was used but there wasn't always the help to get through the schoolwork, and there wasn't always the belief that education was important, especially for women. Find out what things were like when your mom was a child—what were there expectations for her to be educated… were her parents educated… what were some of the things she loved about it… what were some of the issues she came up against…

Did your mom go to school?

If yes, how old was your mom when she started school?

Where did she go to school? Was it very far away?

How did she get to school? Who took her? Who picked her up? Did she have to board with another family?

What did she like about school? What did she dislike about school?

What were some of the rules she had to follow in school?

Highest grade she completed? If she didn't finish school, why not?

Favorite subject in elementary? Why?

Favorite subject in junior high? Why?

Favorite subject in high school? Why?

Least favorite subject in elementary? Why?

Least favorite subject in junior high? Why?

Least favorite subject in high school? Why?

Her favorite teacher? Why?

Her least favorite teacher? Why?

Her best friend in elementary? How did they meet? What things did they do together?

Her best friend in junior high? How did they meet? What things did they do together?

Her best friend in high school? How did they meet? What things did they do together?

Did she ever get into trouble at school? Why? What happened?

Did she do any extra-curricular activities? Sports? Music? Art? Was it her choice?

Does she still do any of the activities she learned while growing up, today?

Was she encouraged to go to school? To do well in school? Did that change as she got into higher grades?

How important does she feel high school education is?

Were there any school dances? Or events?

What did she have for books? Pens/pencils and paper?

Was there a lot of homework? Did she ever have to do it by candlelight?

What did she want to be? Or do?

Or did she take her schooling by correspondence?

Post Secondary/Trades/Training

Did she go on to post secondary? Trades? Or further training?

Was she supported by her parents? Teachers? Community? Siblings?

How did she pay for it?

What did she take? Where did she have to go? Was it close or far away? Did she make it home often or see her family very much?

Did she like what she took? Did she graduate from it?

How important does she feel further education—post secondary, trades, training...—is?

What were some of the issues or problems she ran into, in getting her education?

What did she want to be? Or do?

Did she use her education?

How important does she feel post secondary school is, today?

Notes/Stories

Notes/Stories

Notes/Stories

Notes/Stories

Notes/Stories

Notes/Stories

Chapter 17

Career/Work/Volunteer

Understanding her work/career/volunteering, is an important conversation because she may have wanted to work but it wasn't expected or in some cases women were outright told they couldn't. Do you know about that part of her life? Did she work... Was it accepted... Did she enjoy it... Volunteering was seen differently and was often something that was encouraged and to some degree was expected.

If your mom did NOT work.

If your mom did not work outside of the house, what were things she enjoyed doing around the house? Not enjoy?

What did she keep herself busy with? Especially when the kids were gone to school?

Did she have any free time? What did she do during her free time?

Had she ever wanted to work outside of the home? If yes, what would she have liked to do?

If your mom did work.

Did your mom work outside of the home? If yes, what did she do?

Did she ever change jobs?

Did she have a career?

How did she feel about working? Why did she work?

What were her responsibilities at work?

Did she move up the chain of management?

What did she enjoy about her job?

What did she enjoy least about her job?

Who was the best boss she ever had? What made them good?

Who was the worst boss she ever had? What made them the worst?

Did she get to do the job she always wanted to?

Did she get paid well for what she did? Was her pay inline with what people were being paid at the time?

Did she ever have any free time? What did she do in her free time?

Volunteer work

Did your mom ever volunteer? If yes for what? How did she
end up volunteering for it? Did she enjoy it?

Did she do a lot of volunteering?

What does she think about volunteering?

Notes/Stories

Notes/Stories

Notes/Stories

Chapter 18

Health

Your health is something that is so important but how to take care of it has changed a fair bit over the years. There are a lot of ideas out there on how best to look after yourself and when you go back in time there was a lot less use and emphasis on the medical system, people took care of their own health care—some did it well and some not so well. When your mom was young, things were probably done very differently than now. There might have been limited access to any medical health care—there might not have been a hospital nearby and there might not have been a doctor in the area. So what did they do for their health?

What were some of the things your mom was taught or shown about taking care of herself, when she was young? What did she learn from her parents? What remedies did they use to use? Did she use any of those on you as a child?

Did anyone in her family go to the doctor? The hospital? If yes, why? What was that experience like? Was there someone else they used to go to for health issues? Or just manage the issues, themselves?

What were some of the remedies or health care things, your mom used and has learned along the way?

What was access to medical care like when she was a child vs when you were children vs now?

How has her health been throughout her life? as a child? Tween? Teen? in her 20's? 30's? 40's? 50's? 60's? 70's? 80'? 90's? 100's?

Any diseases? Illnesses? Injuries?

If yes, when? How did it come about? How was it treated?

Did she ever have a real scare with her health? As a child? Tween? Teen? in her 20's? 30's? 40's? 50's? 60's? 70's? 80'? 90's? 100's?

What were some remedies her parents used to use? Did her parents ever have to treat an injury or illness? What did they do? How did that turn out?

Did she ever see a doctor as a child? Did he make house calls?

Has she ever been in the hospital? Have surgery?

What worked best for her in looking after her health?

Was there a remedy she believed helped her when she was sick? If yes what was it?

What did she do to keep healthy?

What does she think about exercise? How important is it to your health?

What does she feel is important to know about health and how to keep healthy today?

Notes/Stories

Notes/Stories

Notes/Stories

Chapter 19

Wealth

Some people have very little or no money growing up, while others grow up with a moderate amount and others grow up quite wealthy. We all strive to make enough income, so we can live a decent life. Some endeavour to make a lot of money in their lives, it becomes their focus, while others see money as the 'root of all evil'. Today, our system is very much about buying and selling, so it is important to have at least some money to make it by in our society.

For a large part of our history though, many found a way around using cash — sometimes by choice and sometimes by circumstances — but they used a barter or trade system. They'd give something they had to get something they wanted. It actually is still used a fair bit today but the majority of what we do is about using money to buy what we need. Do you know what beliefs your mom grew up with around money?

What was your mom's journey with money and how does she feel about it today?

What did her parents teach her about money?

What were her thoughts about money when she was a child? Tween? Teenager? Adult? How has her thoughts about money changed over the years?

Did she grow up with money?

Was she allowed to have money?

Did her parents ever barter or trade services? Did she ever do that?

Has money always been a struggle? Or has it come easily?

When did she get her first bank account? Or did she have one?

Did she work and earn her own money?

Did she ever save money for something?

Did she ever keep a coin because it was special?

Does she feel she was paid fairly for her jobs/career?

Did she feel she had enough money throughout her life?

What was the most extravagant thing she ever bought? What was the most extravagant thing she ever bought for herself?

Did she ever spend money on herself?

What is something she wanted to buy for herself but never did?

Did she ever buy or spend money on something whimsical?

Was she the one to manage the money for the household? If yes, how did she do that? What was her system? Or did she have nothing to do with money? If not, what does she know about how much money they made? Or where that money came from?

Does she worry about money? More or less now than when she was young?

Notes/Stories

Notes/Stories

Notes/Stories

Chapter 20

Travel

Deciding to take a trip today is no big deal. It is quite easy-you hop in your car and drive to where you want to go or you go online and with a few clicks you've booked and paid for your trip and have your tickets. This has changed a lot over the years and continues to change. The how, when, where and the convenience of booking our travel is so much easier, more convenient and faster, never mind the methods of travelling. We can pretty much travel to anywhere in the world without too much difficulty.

Did she ever travel? As a child? Tween? Teen? Adult? On her own? With her parents? Siblings? With a friend? With her spouse? With you, her children?

Where did she travel to? Has she ever traveled far from home? Out of her own state/province? Country? Continent?

How did she travel? What did it cost?

What place did she love the most?

Where would she love to visit again?

What place did she not enjoy?

Did she ever have a crazy experience while traveling? Where was she going? What happened?

What are the different ways in which she has traveled in her lifetime? (i.e. horse, on foot, train, horse and wagon, boat, bus, plane, car, tractor, truck, motorcycle...)

What is the most unique way she ever traveled (i.e. horse and buggy, camel, small airplane, etc.)?

Did she ever drive on any of her trips?

What was the neatest thing she ever learned on one of her trips?

What was the oddest thing she ever learned on one of her trips?

Who was the most memorable person she met from her travels?

What types of food has she tried? What were her favorites? What were things she didn't like? What was the oddest thing she ever ate?

Did she ever get sick or injured while traveling? What happened? How was it treated?

Did she ever have to end a trip early? Why?

Did she ever go camping? Where? With whom? How did she camp—built her own shelter, cabin, tent, trailer...?

Was she ever caught in any historical events?

What is her favorite memory of the places she's been to?

Is there one place she thinks you should travel to?

Notes/Stories

Notes/Stories

Notes/Stories

Chapter 21

Beliefs

The way we see and understand the world and ourselves really makes all the difference for where we go, what we do and where we end up. Our beliefs direct our lives often in ways we don't understand. Our beliefs are changing and being challenged all the time.

How did your mom see the world as a child? Tween? Teen? In her 20's? 30's? 40's? 50's? 60's? 70's? 80'? 90's? 100's?

What are the things she remembers about how she thought life would be?

What did she believe her life would look like?

What are the beliefs she has held about herself her whole life? (good and bad)

What are the beliefs she struggled with about herself as a teen? In her 20's? 30's? 40's? 50's? 60's? 70's? 80'? 90's? 100's?

How did she handle change? What are some major changes she made in her life? Why? How did they turn out?

How does she think her beliefs have directed her life?

What was her biggest fear about her life?

What does she believe is her greatest accomplishment?

Notes/Stories

Notes/Stories

Notes/Stories

Notes/Stories

Chapter 22

Dreams/Aspirations/Goals

*Y*our mom has or had dreams and aspirations. This is where you get to discover what she wanted in her life and whether she achieved them, made strides toward achieving them or just kept them to herself.

As a little girl, what did she want to be when she grew up? Did she do it? If she did was it what she thought it would be? If not, why not? What did she do instead?

What are some of the dreams she had? Did she achieve any of them? Did she try?
As a teen? In her 20's? 30's? 40's? 50's? 60's? 70's? 80'? 90's? 100's?

If she did work towards living her dream, what were some of the problems or issues she encountered along the way?

If she didn't live some of her dreams or reach some of her goals, what does she believe kept her from achieving them?

What does she now see differently and wished she'd known earlier in life?

What is she happiest about in her life?

What is her biggest regret? What does she wish she had done? Or done differently?

What is her greatest learning?

What is she most proud of in her life?

What advice would she give young women of today about work? About family? About life?

Notes/Stories

Notes/Stories

Notes/Stories

Notes/Stories

Chapter 23

Favorite Hobbies/Artistic Endeavors/Sports/ Clubs/Memberships

Favorite Things to Do
Hobbies, Sports, Music, Art, Writing, Dancing, Clubs, Memberships...

We all have hobbies, sports, music, artistic endeavors, etc. that we enjoy. Sometimes we continue to do them throughout life but sometimes we don't. Sometimes we stop doing one activity and start a new one. What we do or enjoy often changes over time. Now you can discover what were some things your mom used to do, why she did them and if she continued or quit doing them. Do you know if she was involved in any clubs or held any memberships?

What was her favorite hobby to do as a child? Tween? Teen? 20's? 30's? 40's? 50's? 60's? 70's? 80's? 90's? 100's?

What was her favorite sport to do as a child? Tween? Teen? 20's? 30's? 40's? 50's? 60's? 70's? 80's? 90's? 100's?

What was her favorite music to play as a child? Tween? Teen? 20's? 30's? 40's? 50's? 60's? 70's? 80's? 90's? 100's?

What was her favorite music to listen to as a child? Tween? Teen? 20's? 30's? 40's? 50's? 60's? 70's? 80's? 90's? 100's?

What was her favorite song to listen to as a child? Tween? Teen? 20's? 30's? 40's? 50's? 60's? 70's? 80's? 90's? 100's?

What was her favorite type of art or crafts to do as a child? Tween? Teen? 20's? 30's? 40's? 50's? 60's? 70's? 80's? 90's? 100's?

What was her creative talent? Did she ever paint? Write? Dance? Sing? Sculpt? Play music? Other?

What is something she has done that shocked people? When did she do it? Why?

Who did she like to do activities with as a child? Tween? Teen? 20's? 30's? 40's? 50's? 60's? 70's? 80's? 90's? 100's?

Was she ever part of a club? If yes, what was the club and what did they do? How did she become involved with this group?

Did she hold any memberships? If yes, to what? Why did she join?

Did she play games as a child? Adult? What was her favorite game? Board game?

Did she spend much time in nature? Outdoors? What did she like to do outdoors?

Notes/Stories

Notes/Stories

Notes/Stories

Notes/Stories

Notes/Stories

Chapter 24

Tough Times

We all go through a lot in our lifetime, some things are easy, some are fun, some just happen but some of the things that happen just aren't all that easy to get through. In our lifetime we deal with issues in all areas of our lives from health, money, beliefs about ourselves, to relationships to death. Just imagine how much your mom has seen in her lifetime. She has seen and been through a lot. Are you aware of what many of those issues would be?

What were some tough things she had to deal with in her life? (maybe to do with family, health, marriage, children, aging, community, friends, relatives, lack of resources, housing/ accommodations, loss of loved ones, loss of some thing...)

What were some of those things that she came up against as she went through life... As a child? Tween? Teen? In her 20's? 30's? 40's? 50's? 60's? 70's? 80'? 90's? 100's?

How did she handle each situation? How does she think it changed her moving forward? What did she learn to believe from that situation? How did others see those situations?

What kept her moving forward?

Did she ever struggle with managing money? With where the next dollar would come from?

Did she ever struggle with putting enough food on the table? With ensuring you, her kids, had what they needed?

What is her advice for getting through tough situations?

Notes/Stories

Notes/Stories

Notes/Stories

Notes/Stories

Chapter 25

Friends

Through our lifetime we meet many people. Your mom has probably met a lot of people throughout her life. Some will have left a lasting impression, some positive and some not so positive. Some of those she has met will have become casual friends while others will have become good friends. Who were some of those people who have passed through your mom's life? Who were those people who impacted her in a positive way?

Who was her best friend as a child? Teen? 20's? 30's? 40's? 50's? 60's? 70's? 80's? 90's? 100's?

What were some things she and her best friend used to do? To talk about?

How did her and her best friend meet?

Who were some of her friends, throughout her life? How did she meet them? What were things they liked to do?

Has she kept in touch with any of her friends over the years?

Are any of her friends still alive?

Who did she talk to when she had problems? As a child? Teen? 20's? 30's? 40's? 50's? 60's? 70's? 80's? 90's? 100's?

Did she ever have any pen-pals? Who? How long did she stay in touch? Did they ever meet in person?

Did she find it easy or hard to make friends throughout her life?

Who are some of her friends now? What do they like to do together?

What does being a friend mean to her?

Notes/Stories

Notes/Stories

Notes/Stories

Notes/Stories

Chapter 26

Raising You

*H*aving a baby is an amazing journey. Today it is so much more open and embraced and celebrated. If you're mom had you before the 70's, things were quite different then. People were still happy about their being a baby but the experience wasn't so openly shared. It would be well worth finding out what it was like for your mom.

Often, we don't ask questions about how we came to be. Sometimes we hear different stories throughout our life but we never really ask in a moment of good rapport and when we are really paying attention to the facts. Why does it matter? Because too often, things are said at sensitive times or when emotions are high and then they can become misunderstood. There is also this belief that all women just naturally know how to have babies and how to raise them. Unfortunately, that isn't true. Some women really like being pregnant and the whole experience, while others don't. Some women seem to have a natural instinct about raising children, while others don't.

I know my mom, who had seven pregnancies, did not want children. Does that mean she didn't love me or my siblings? No. It meant that growing up she did not understand kids or what being around kids meant. She was scared that she didn't and couldn't relate to children. She grew up mostly around adults. Her brother was 9 years older than she was, so she had very little experience hanging out with other children her own age. She had almost no involvement with babies.

I could have held onto the fact that she didn't want children, didn't want me, but that wasn't true. She may have said she didn't want to have wanted kids and I think at times she felt a bit lost as to what to do with all of us. I do know however, that she loved us deeply and wanted so much for us. I don't ever remember her saying 'I love you', at least when I was a child, but she did many things that were her way of showing she loved us. That of course took me a while to understand but when I did, it helped to shift how I saw her and all that she had done for us as children. I can still smell and taste her cinnamon buns… cookies… special dishes… I can still see her making clothes for us… I still remember the things she taught us… I still hear her shooing us outside to enjoy the sun and outdoors…

Education was always a big thing for her, especially for her five daughters. She herself had gotten an education — she was one of 2 women to graduate in a class of 126. Pretty impressive to me. She knew there was something more for each of us, so she encouraged us to do more… be more...

I finally sat down with her and talked with her about her life, the choices she'd made and about having kids. We had some amazing conversations. I am forever grateful that I took that leap and talked with her about her life. It gave me a whole new perspective on who she was and all that she'd tried to do for us. I also finally understood that all the things she did for us — made, cooked, sewed, or the things she got us involved in — were her way of expressing her love. She did learn to say 'I love you' when we were adults. So I did get to hear those words before she passed away. And she got to hear those words from my siblings and myself, many times. Even writing this I can hear her correcting my English—such a beautiful memory. It was important to her how we, her children, showed up because she wanted others to see us how she did and to know how good we were as people.

She raised us the best way she knew how. Did she get it all right? No, but I do know there were things she did well and some things maybe not so well. But she did try to provide for us what she thought would make us good people and to be able to take care of ourselves. She taught us how to be strong, independent individuals. What a gift.

Your Mom raised kids in a time when you didn't really talk about your personal struggles with being a mom.... With how difficult you found it.... The things that went well... The things that didn't go well.... You really kept a lot of that to yourself. And I think it is somewhat still true for today. We may share some of the things we've found that work but we really don't talk about feeling scared or that we feel we're messing up or maybe that we're really not sure all the time what we're doing. It is not an easy role in life but it is and can be one of the most rewarding.

Raising kids is work and it means as a Mom you may give up a lot. And when we are talking about raising kids, 40-50-60+ years ago, she gave up so much time, energy, and dreams to raise them. This doesn't mean she regrets it, it just means it was different times. She may not have had the opportunity to have a life of her own.

Talk to your mom, not when things are happening but when there is a quiet moment and when you have a good rapport with her. Go with an open mind and listen as though listening to someone you don't know. Because in all honesty I bet you may not really know the woman you call Mom. Embrace what she tells you, listen and try to get the context of the times.

Pregnancy

What was her pregnancy like when she carried you? Your siblings? Any complications?

What was your birth like? Your siblings? Any complications? Where were you born? Where were your siblings born?

How did your parents choose your name? Your siblings' names?

What was it like when you were born? Were a lot of women choosing not to have children? Were women starting to step outside the norm — work and/or get educated?

What kind of medical support was there? Did she ever need any?

Was your dad able to be present? Or anyone else?

After you were born, how did your mom carry you around — in a sling? In her arms?...? or did she?

Did she have a stroller or buggy? Did they have car seats?

Did she have a high chair for you? Or stack books for you to sit on?

How many pregnancies did she have?

What kind of food did your mom feed you as a baby? Toddler? Child?

What kind of clothes did you wear as a baby? Toddler? Child? Where did she get your clothes (i.e. hand-me downs, at a store, sewed them…)?

What was something special she liked to do with you as a baby? Toddler? Child?

Raising You

What were her goals for you? How did she see you as a child? What were her hopes and dreams for you? For your siblings?

What does she feel she did well? What are things she wished she could do differently?

What does she now know that she wished she'd known then?

What is her biggest realization about raising you? Your siblings?

What did she realize about each of you? Was it very different to raise each one of you?

Did she ever get a babysitter? Who was the person? When did they babysit?

Were there ever any incidents with the babysitter? What happened?

How did she manage raising you (and your siblings) and do all the work she had to do?

What is one thing available today that she wished she had back then?

What was and is the best part of being a Mom?

Did your mom work while you were a baby? A child? Tween? Teen? How did she manage everything?
What were special dishes she used to make you? Or a favorite treat?

Did she ever make you sweets or candy?

What were some of the things she used to make for you (i.e. clothes, blankets, toys, crafts...)?

What did she tell you about the opposite sex? What did she tell you about dating? Marriage? What did she want for you in regards to a relationship? Children?

What were some fun things you used to do together? What did she love doing with you?

What did she enjoy teaching you?

What did she feel it was important for you to know? How did she feel it was important to show up?

Who did she talk to when she was overwhelmed? Did she feel that raising you was mostly on her shoulders?

What is she proudest of in raising you?

Your Health (you or your siblings)

What were some things she did in looking after your health as a child? i.e. when you got the flu, what did she do to treat it?

How did she treat colds? The flu?

Did you or your siblings ever get really sick? Injured? Were any of you sick very much?

Was there anything special she had to do because of your or your siblings health?

What was and is her best advice on how to take care of your health?

How did she see being physically active? Did she feel it was important?

Did she feel it was important that you get outside every day or as often as possible?

Your Career

What did she want for you for work or a career? Did she feel it was important?

What did she want for your siblings for work or a career?

Other

What did she want for you, in regard to education?

What did she want for you in life?

What did she want you to know about money?

Did you ever have pets when you were young? Did she like having pets around?

What is she happiest about with raising you and your siblings?

What are all of your siblings full names and ages?

Did you ever attend a special event—show, concert...?

Did you ever have family get togethers or family reunions? If yes, who'd all attend?

Did they ever have neighborhood/community get togethers? Or picnics?

Notes/Stories

Notes/Stories

Notes/Stories

Notes/Stories

Notes/Stories

Chapter 27

The Best Things
You Learned from your Mom

Her Advice

What are those things she used to tell you, those things you heard but maybe took for granted or kind of brushed off as I've heard this before or yeah, I get it... but now you realize how wise they were... how fun they were... how eye opening they were...

This is a list of the things you and your siblings have learned from your mom that has helped you the most. Those words of wisdom, funny things she used to say, how she approached certain situations, the positive way she treated people... All those neat things she either taught you or she demonstrated through who she was and is.

What were her words of wisdom?

How did she approach stressful situations?

How did she approach difficult situations?

How did she approach people in general?

How did she approach difficult people?

What was something funny she used to say?

What was some neat things she used to do for others?

About Life
What is her best advice about life?

Being happy
What does she believe makes her happy? What does she believe would keep you happy?

Dreams/Goals
What is her best advice about going for your dreams and goals?

Education
What is her advice about getting further education?

Career
What was her view or expectation for a career for you?

Relationships
What makes a good relationship? How do you keep a good relationship?

Family
What is her advice about family? What does it take to make a family happy? The best way to raise kids? The best thing to teach them?

Other

What advice did she always give you growing up?

What did she always say to you growing up?

What was her best advice overall?

What doe she feel is the best part about aging?

What is her fondest memory?

What were some of those things that she kept telling you about life as a child? Tween? Teen? Adult?

Notes/Stories

Notes/Stories

Notes/Stories

Notes/Stories

Notes/Stories

Chapter 28

Favorite Recipes, Patterns, How To's

There are those things we remember eating as kids that make us always think of Mom—fresh bread, cinnamon buns, cookies, casseroles, a special dish, a dip, jams, pickles... It's also those fun things she made for us to play with or that she made to use—playdough, coloring for Easter eggs, stain remover, soap... Or the things she made for us to wear or use—knit, crochet, do needlepoint, sew... Or the things she used to build or make... Or the crafts or hobbies she used to do...

There are so many things our moms teach us, so many things we take for granted and often think, 'I'll just ask Mom'. But there will be a day she won't be able to tell you anymore. This is a great time and a great place to write down those things she has taught you that you really want to remember and keep for the future.

What were some of her favorite recipes?

What were yours?

What were some of the things she made for you to play with
as a child (i.e. playdough, color for Easter eggs…)? How did
she make them? Tween? Teen? Adult?

What were some of the things she made and used? Or made
for you to use?

Did she used to sew or do needlepoint, crochet, knit…? Was
there a pattern that she used to use that you'd like to learn? Or
to keep?

Did your mom build things, make things or fix things? How
did she do it? What did she use?

What is a dish she used to make? Desserts? Treats? Jams?
Pickles? Specialty dishes?

What was something she used to make that you used as a
child? Tween? Teen? Adult?

What were some of the remedies she used to make?

How did she make…?

What did she used to do when…?

What inspired her to make…?

Notes/Stories

Notes/Stories

Notes/Stories

Notes/Stories

Chapter 29

Family History and Stories

*H*ere you can keep track of your family history. Who are the people who make up your past and what are some of the stories about those people your mom is always talking about. Do a simple family tree so you remember who was who and how they are related. Also keep track of any information you might want to remember about them.

If you're unsure how to create a family tree, here are some ideas for how to create them and the information you might want to document. How far back in your family history you want to go is up to you. You might also want to include more information about who each of your ancestors were—where they lived, worked, some stories about their lives. Have fun with this.

Format 1:

Grandparents name and date of birth and where born.

Their children's (your mom and your aunts and uncles) names and dates of birth

Their children's (you, your siblings, your cousins) names and dates of birth

Format 2:

Grandparents (names and date of birth)

Their Children (mom and siblings names and dates of birth)

Their Children (You and your cousins names and dates of birth)

Family Tree

Notes/Stories

Chapter 30

Religion/Spirituality

This is another area many say not to have a conversation about but it can be quite interesting to know what your mom's views are on religion and spirituality. What was she taught as a child, what was she raised to believe and how or if that has changed over time?

Was she raised in a religious or spiritual household?

What were some of their religious or spiritual practices?

What is her belief about religion? About spirituality? Has that changed over the years?

What are her religious or spiritual practices today?

What did she feel was important that you, her children understood about religion or spirituality when you were young? Now?

What is important to her about religion? Spirituality?

When she dies what does she believe will happen to her?

What does she want for a funeral?

Notes/Stories

Notes/Stories

Chapter 31

Politics

olitics is often another subject many want to stay away from, however it would be good to know your mom's view on this topic.

What were her political views growing up? What are they now?

What does she think of the politics of today?

Did she vote throughout her life? Why? Or why not?

Does she see voting as important? Why? Or why not?

Was she ever involved in politics?

What does she want you to know about politics?

Did she ever get involved in politics?

Did she ever get into arguments over politics?

Who does she believe is the best leader in politics that she has seen in her lifetime?

Does she think you should be more involved in politics and what is going on?

Notes/Stories

Notes/Stories

Chapter 32

Your Memories

ere you can keep track of the memories you have of your mom, those special moments in your life when she was there for you. Or those cool things you know she did.

What are favorite things she did for you as a child?

Your favorite smell that reminds you of her?

A flower that reminds you of her?

A food that reminds you of her?

An activity you enjoyed doing together?

A joke between you?

A song you both enjoyed?

A place you liked to visit?

A show you both loved to watch?

A favorite dessert that she made?

Something she did that you hold dear?

Something she said that you hold dear?

How you see her growing up? Now?

What are some mementos that remind you of your mom? Or a special time?

Notes/Stories

Notes/Stories

Notes/Stories

Notes/Stories

Chapter 33

Keep the Conversations Going

The truth is we all go through good times and we all go through hard times at some point or other in our life. The interesting thing about those difficult times is whether you are able to put them in perspective and move on without those things keeping you down, angry or bitter. The best piece of advice I can give is to reframe those situations and to come from a place of gratitude. Be thankful for every day and every event, find the positive and discover what you can learn from it but don't hold onto the anger. Look for the good, look for what will help you moving forward… and move on. If you are struggling with this, find someone, maybe a mentor, coach, or other professional, who can help you to understand and to reframe your relationship. It is time to grow, mend and heal.

My hope is that you'll be able to create a stronger, more loving bond but I do know that it is not possible in all cases. For your benefit though, put your Mom and her life into perspective, in relationship to yours. She did what she knew with what she had. It might have been enough but it might not have been. She did not act the way she did to hurt you, she did it because she didn't know any other way. Love her and forgive her, it will help you to heal.

The key to connecting with your mom, is to meet her where she is at. What are the things that have meaning for her? What are the things with which you can connect with her? As I've mentioned throughout the book, try to find those things she relates to and step into her world. When you can, share your experiences as well.

If your mom is struggling with talking about herself or her life, help her see the good of who she is and all she has done. Help her to see the positive that has come out of her life. She is an amazing woman, one who has flaws and quirks and hang-ups, like the rest of us. She may need help seeing how important she is and that she matters. Honor your mom. But also honor yourself, recognize who you are. Know that you can put the past into perspective and reframe how you see it. Remember this is about moving forward so you can be happy, know you mattered and feel connected and loved. And hopefully you can help your mom achieve that as well.

Use this journey of exploring her history, to understand her and to keep those conversations going.

There are some extra blank pages where you can keep track of the additional stories she tells. It might be about how she came to live where she is… more about her parents… her siblings… her journey… some special moments in her life… some traumatic moments her life… some neat things she learned… how she views the world… any vices she might have had… Something she tried for the fun of it…

Notes/Stories

Notes/Stories

Notes/Stories

Notes/Stories

Notes/Stories

Notes/Stories

Notes/Stories

Notes/Stories

Notes/Stories

Notes/Stories

Mom...

A mixture of

sprinkles of fairy dust and magic

milk and cookies

sternness and discipline

hope and laughter

and love...

Thank you for reading **Do You Know Your Mom's Story? 365 Questions You Need to Ask Her.**

I hope you enjoyed reading it as much as I enjoyed writing it. **Please leave a review on the online bookstores, it helps others to find it.**

Recommend this book to family and friends, coworkers, women and men everywhere—help them to document their mom's life and hopefully to also grow, mend or heal their relationships with their mom's.

I'd love to hear from you, how you are finding connecting with your mom, what you've learned and anything about this journey that you'd like to share. And if you come up with more questions to you ask your mom I'd love to hear them.

Email me at mom@glennamageau.com

Websites: www.glennamageau.com and www.womenwritesmovement.com

Email: mom@glennamageau.com

About the Author

Glenna is a multi-award-winning author, speaker and coach. Her passion is to empower and inspire women to discover who they are and to explore their gifts and talents. In writing this novel, her goal is to help women go into old age with knowing they mattered, were loved and feel connected. It is also meant to help children to grow, mend or heal their relationship with their moms.

Glenna is also the founder of the Women Writes Movement — helping women find their voice through writing.

To learn more: www.glennamageau.com

Other Books by Glenna Mageau

Nonfiction

Don't Laugh a Woman's Playbook to the U-R-In Line for the
Women's Public Bathroom Again!

Fiction - Suspense/Thrillers (under the penname Maggie Thom)

The Caspian Wine Series
    Captured Lies
    Deceitful Truths
    Split Seconds

Other Suspense/Thriller Fiction
    Tainted Waters
    Deadly Ties

9 781775 269816